BEHAVING BADLY?
IRISH MIGRANTS AND CRIME IN THE VICTORIAN CITY

Roger Swift

Professor of Victorian Studies

An Inaugural Lecture
Delivered at Chester College of Higher Education
on 23 November 2000

Chester Academic Press

First published 2006
by Chester Academic Press
Corporate Communications
University of Chester
Parkgate Road
Chester CH1 4BJ

Printed and bound in the UK by the
Learning Resources Print Unit,
University of Chester
Cover designed by the
Learning Resources Graphics Team
University of Chester

©Roger Swift, 2006

All Rights Reserved
No part of this publication may be reproduced, stored in a retrieval system or transmitted in any form or by any means without the prior permission of the copyright owner, other than as permitted by current UK legislation or under the terms of a recognised copyright licensing scheme

A catalogue record for this publication is available from the British Library

BEHAVING BADLY?
IRISH MIGRANTS AND CRIME IN THE VICTORIAN CITY

The first half of the nineteenth century witnessed a substantial increase in the pace and scale of Irish migration to Britain. The 1841 Census enumerated the Irish-born population of England, Wales and Scotland at 419,000 and by 1851, in consequence of the massive exodus during the Great Famine, this figure had risen to 727,000. In 1861, the Irish-born population peaked at 806,000, when it comprised 3.5% of the total population. Thereafter, as migration from Ireland to Britain declined, the number of Irish-born migrants in Britain also progressively fell, declining to 550,000 (or 1.3% of the population) in 1911. In essence, this process involved the positive movement of people in search of better economic opportunities in Britain and, accordingly, the Irish presence was concentrated overwhelmingly in the towns and cities of "the workshop of the world". These migrants, many of whom subsequently re-emigrated, were by no means an homogeneous group, for their ranks contained both rich and poor, middle class and working class, skilled and unskilled, Catholics and Protestants (as well as un-believers), Nationalists and Loyalists, and men and women from a variety of distinctive provincial rural and urban cultures in Ireland. The majority were young, single people, disproportionately male. They were also notoriously transient, and the urban districts they inhabited experienced continual in- and out-migration, with only a relatively small number of migrants establishing permanent settlements. But the vast majority of these Irish people were poor and they were Roman Catholics, and it is their story - a story, in many cases, of triumph over adversity - that looms large in the history of the Irish in Britain.[1]

The Irish presence was generally unpopular and, even before the Famine, British social investigators and commentators variously perceived Irish migration as little short of a social disaster which, it was argued, exacerbated urban squalor, constituted a health hazard, and increased the burden on the Poor Rates. It was also argued that the Irish constituted a threat to law and order in British cities. In 1836, the *Report on the State of the Irish Poor in Great Britain* devoted four pages to the examination of Irish criminality, noting that "... the Irish in the larger towns of Lancashire commit more crimes than an equal number of natives of the same places".[2] In 1839, the *Report of the Constabulary Commissioners* concluded that, in the towns of South Lancashire, "... when large bodies of Irish of less orderly habits, and far more prone to the use of violence in fits of intoxication settled permanently in these towns, the existing police force, which was sufficient to repress crime and disorders among a purely English population, has been found, under these altered circumstances, inadequate to the regular enforcement of the law".[3] In the same year, Thomas Carlyle, the intellectual hero of the age, was moved to comment: "Crowds of miserable Irish darken all our towns ... as the ready-made nucleus of degradation and disorder",[4] whilst in 1854 a Leicester clergyman observed of the Irish: "They are a great calamity to our large towns. Wherever they locate they introduce crime, disease, and wretchedness".[5] Similar observations were also expressed by some foreign visitors to England during the 1840s.[6] Of course, these are random examples, but they are illustrative of a more popular belief in the innate criminality of the Irish poor, which formed part of the negative side of the Irish stereotype. Indeed, to many middle-class observers, Irish migrants augmented a challenge by the "dangerous classes" to authority and order in urban Britain.

Relatively few detailed analyses of the Irish contribution to Victorian crime rates have been conducted by historians. This said, the chief conclusion to be drawn from selective local studies of crime (which may therefore be unrepresentative) in some early and mid-Victorian towns, including York, Manchester, Liverpool, Preston, Bradford, Wolverhampton, Chester and Middlesbrough, is that the Irish-born were not only well represented in the statistics of crime, but that their capacity for breaking the law was disproportionate to their numbers in the community at large.[7] These studies conclude that the Irish-born were almost three times as likely to face prosecution than their English neighbours, endorsing the evidence of policemen, prison officers, and magistrates contained in the *Report on the State of the Irish Poor in Great Britain* of 1836.[8] However, these statistics deserve further scrutiny. Firstly, they refer only to the Irish-born and do not include the children of Irish immigrants born in Britain who, though perceived by the host society as Irish, were variously classified as English, Scottish or Welsh. Thus, the contribution of the Irish to local criminality was probably higher than these figures suggest. Secondly, the Irish proportion of the working-class population of these towns was obviously far higher than its proportion of the population as a whole, and the statistics reflect to some extent the relatively high proportion of Irish in that sector of society most likely to be prosecuted.[9] Thirdly, many of the second and third generation Irish would have been Roman Catholics and hence the proportion of Catholics in the statistics of crime would have been higher than those of the Irish. Fourthly, these localised surveys suggest that the proportion of Irish-born enumerated in the statistics of crime gradually declined towards the end of the nineteenth century. This does not imply that the Irish were less likely to face prosecution (for they continued to be over-represented); it merely reflects, in relative terms, the decline in immigration from Ireland and the consequent reduction in the number of Irish-born in Britain during the period. Finally, it is important to recognise that the incidence of crime, both Irish and non-Irish, was in reality much higher than the statistics of crime (which are notoriously unreliable) imply, for they represent only those offences which were reported to the police and which resulted in prosecutions and convictions, as opposed to all offences committed, many of which went unreported (the so-called "dark figure of crime"). The Irish-born were also over-represented in committals to prison during the nineteenth century. The *Judicial Statistics* for England and Wales for the period 1861-1901 indicate that, whilst the proportion of Irish-born prisoners gradually declined, the Irish-born were five times more likely to be committed to prison than the English.[10] Thus, on the surface at least, the criminal statistics suggest that the Irish were more likely to be prosecuted and convicted for law-breaking than their English, Scottish or Welsh neighbours.

Moreover, the evidence suggests that it was not just a case of men behaving badly, for Irish women also figure disproportionately in the statistics of crime.[11] To take but one example, in Chester between 1851 and 1871, Irish women comprised 67% of female convictions for assaults on the police, 28% for assault, 33% for obtaining goods by false pretences, 33% for begging and 23% for drunkenness and disorderly behaviour.[12] Notable among these women was Mary Ann Glynn of Boughton, who carried 101 convictions for drunkenness, disorderly behaviour, vagrancy and petty thefts. Sentenced to imprisonment for twelve months in July 1869, she continued to defy authority in Chester Gaol, using "obscene and violent language" and subsequently destroying "… 13 panes of glass, 2 cell stools, 1 lamp, 8 beds, 10 jackets, 12 petticoats, 19 capes, 2 blankets, 6 chemises, 2 flannel ivylets, 6 tin cans and 2 chamber utensils". A muff (restraining jacket) was duly deployed to control her, but to little effect.[13] But even Glynn's record pales into insignificance when compared with that of one Liverpool Irish woman, a street trader, who by 1897 boasted a national record, having been held 356 times for drunkenness, assaults, damage and begging.[14]

However, these patterns require further qualification. Firstly, there is much evidence to suggest that Irish criminality was concentrated largely in less serious or petty categories. The *Report on the State of the Irish Poor* concluded that: "Crimes against the person, committed after long premeditation and with unrelenting cruelty, by several persons, such as murders, nightly attacks on houses, beatings, vindictive rapes, &c., which are unhappily so frequent among the Irish in their own country, scarcely ever occur among them in Great Britain",[15] and police superintendents in Liverpool and Manchester told a similar story.[16] Some local studies of Irish crime have confirmed this impression, by showing that whilst the Irish were over-represented in prosecutions at the local Petty Sessions, they were less frequently committed to the Quarter Sessions and Assizes.[17] Secondly, the evidence suggests that the Irish were not over-represented in all categories of petty crime. As I have shown elsewhere,[18] Irish criminality was highly concentrated in the often inter-related categories of drunkenness, disorderly behaviour and assault (including assaults on the police) and, to a lesser extent, petty theft and vagrancy. On average, almost one third of all prosecutions in these categories involved

Irish people. Yet the supposed predilection of the Irish for such offences is deserving of closer scrutiny.

Consider, for example, drink-related crime. In British eyes, the terms "drink" and "Irish" were synonymous.[19] Drink, it was argued, was the Irishman's weakness and drunkenness was the precursor of disorderly behaviour, breaches of the peace of all kinds, and assaults. It was also held that drink had a markedly different effect upon the Irish than their neighbours, prompting a Cardiff magistrate, in reference to excessive drunkenness among Irish dockworkers in 1877, to claim "… they are not all bad fellows, but they have all the peculiarities of their forefathers".[20] This view is perhaps indicative of the way in which contemporaries sometimes resorted to stereotype and conveniently ignored the drunken violence that distinguished English, Scottish and Welsh working-class mores, although even John Denvir, an Irish nationalist, was moved to comment that, whilst the Irish did not drink more than other nationalities, "… being naturally demonstrative, they put themselves in evidence when under the influence of intoxicants, where the Englishman would go and sleep off their effects".[21] Of course, the Irish were far from being inveterate imbibers; located as they were in marginal employments, most Irish people could not afford to drink throughout the week and those who drank confined the practice to the weekend. And while the public houses and beer-shops that proliferated in the working-class districts populated by the Irish poor provided plenty of opportunities for drink, they also served important social, cultural and economic functions for Irish people.[22] Moreover, it was a common practice for contractors to pay Irish labourers their wages in public houses, which not only encouraged them to spend their wages on drink, but also occasioned disputes between labourers and contractors and amongst labourers themselves. Public houses were not, however, the only focus for Irish drinking practices. Some migrants brought alcohol with them from Ireland and sold it, without licence, in local lodging-houses. These "wabble shops" were illegal, but were very difficult for the police to detect.[23] So too were illegal whiskey stills. These were usually located in lodging-houses, and it was reported in 1836 that in Manchester these houses were "… crammed with Irish the whole of Saturday night; parties of men come mad drunk out of these places".[24]

But the realities of Irish drinking were more complex and varied than this imagery suggests. Drink was a key element of leisure culture in rural Ireland and played a central role in the main rituals of life: birth, marriage and death. The consumption of whiskey ("water of life" in Gaelic) was fundamental to this.[25] Yet patterns of drink consumption in Ireland varied according to a variety of influences; rural drinking was irregular, confined largely to weekends and special occasions, whereas urban drinking was more regular and, in some instances, daily. Nevertheless, the persistence of the Irish reputation for drunkenness was based in part on the assumption that expatriate (migrant) drinking habits were also characteristic of Ireland, which was not wholly true. Arguably, as one historian has observed, the key questions which should be addressed to this issue should not be "Why Paddy Drank" (which assumes the validity of the stereotype), but rather "Did Paddy Drink?" (where the evidence suggests both "Yes" and "No") and "Which Paddy Drank?"[26] Indeed, the efforts of temperance crusaders such as Father Mathew met with some success in both Ireland and Britain. Henry Mayhew noted the presence of mutual aid societies, including temperance groups, among London's Irish Catholics in the 1840s, while one of the motives for Mathew's visit to Glasgow in 1842 and to other British towns in 1843 was to raise the reputation - soiled by drink - of the Irish in Britain, sometimes administering the pledge in Gaelic. Thus, "Teetotal Paddy" reflects the other side of the coin.[27] It is also worth noting that, between 1841 and 1871, Irish spirit consumption was actually below the annual United Kingdom average, while beer consumption in England, Scotland and Wales was almost four times higher than in Ireland.[28]

Consider too, the link between the Irish and disorder. This has been the subject of much research, and a closer analysis of Irish disorders suggests that they were essentially multi-causal and came in various shapes and sizes. Sometimes they comprised disturbances among the Irish themselves; on other occasions, they involved collective violence either by the Irish or against the Irish, or a combination of both. Moreover, they operated on both intra-communal and inter-communal levels within specific communities, revealing different types of behaviour according to time and place. For example, disorders that were confined to Irish districts consisted largely of drunken brawls, quarrels between neighbours and domestic disputes. Much of this violence was between rather than against Irish people. When combined with the drunkenness, noise and casual violence associated with Saturday night saturnalia in the public houses, beer-shops and lodging-houses of so-called "Little Irelands" - not to mention the celebration of weddings, wakes and St Patrick's Day - these disorders made the Irish more visible, reinforcing the popular perception of the Irish predilection for drunkenness and disorderly behaviour, and sometimes inviting attention from the police. The Superintendent of the Stockport Police noted in 1836 that: "Very aggravated assaults committed in a state of drunkenness are particularly frequent. They fight with weapons, as firepokers, pieces of iron, or shillelaghs, and rarely with fists. Frequently on these occasions they stab one another: these fights are principally among the Irish of different parties, and not so often between English and Irish; the parties depend on the part of the country whence they came".[29] Yet these "Irish rows", as the provincial press described them and which so horrified "respectable" opinion, were generally of little interest to the police or magistrates, unless they spilled over into the public domain.

By contrast, violence bred of sectarian rivalries sometimes spilled over into the public domain in cities with substantial Ulster Protestant and Irish Catholic populations; most notably - in view of their proximity to Ireland - in the ports of Liverpool and Glasgow. Here, communal conflicts were compounded by the activities of the Orange Order, and Orange marches, an important element in Protestant working-class culture, were frequently accompanied by violence between Catholics and Protestants well into the Edwardian period.[30] In the West of Scotland, sectarian violence also erupted in smaller towns with Irish populations during the mid-Victorian years, including Airdrie, Port Glasgow, Greenock, Dumbarton, Kelso, Coatbridge and Paisley where, in 1857, three members of the local night police, as soon as they were dismissed from duty, joined an Orange procession in their uniforms, carried flags and led an assault on a body of Irish Catholics, one of whom was stabbed to death.[31] In England, sectarian violence also disfigured community relations in the industrial townships of late Victorian Cumbria, including Barrow, Workington, Whitehaven and Cleator Moor.[32] Nevertheless, sectarian conflict appears in general to have been less evident in most Irish communities in nineteenth-century Britain.

Clashes between the Irish and the police had a character of their own. Police attempts in Irish districts to quell intra-communal disorders, to enforce the licensing laws, to trace illegal stills, to regulate lodging-houses and to apprehend suspicious characters were perceived by the Irish as examples of police violence and often led to serious and more generalised disorders,[33] at which point the distinction between "intra-communal" and "inter-communal" violence becomes blurred. For example, the Chief Constable of Wolverhampton reported in 1849 that it was necessary to remove policemen from other parts of the town in order to contain disturbances in the Irish district, noting: "Whenever a disturbance takes place, these overcrowded lodging-houses pour forth their inmates in almost incredible numbers, attacking a single policeman or two with great ferocity and savageness, but being equally expert in beating a retreat when faced by a sufficient force to repel their lawless proceedings".[34] In short, whole Irish communities often stood shoulder to shoulder in face of what they popularly held to be police harassment, and the over-representation of Irish people in statistics pertaining to assaults on the police, which often occurred during these disorders, could be seen in part as an index of Irish hostility to police interference, even though there were also disproportionate numbers of Irishmen in the police force. Thus, it is not surprising to discover that Irish people comprised 33% of all prosecutions for assaults on the police in Liverpool and Manchester between 1841 and 1871,[35] and 20% in Birmingham between 1862 and 1877, although they comprised only 4% of the local population.[36]

It is difficult to lay exclusive blame on either side for some of these inter-communal disorders. There were, for example, some famous battles between Irish and English railway navvies during the 1830s and 1840s, which were in part rooted in the harshness of that kind of life.[37] Yet navvy riots were also multi-causal. In some instances, they involved violence by the Irish as a protest against their exploitation by contractors and gangers; in others, they may be ascribed to English or Scottish xenophobia, which resulted in violence against the Irish. There were, too, instances of navvy violence being manipulated by rival railway companies in order to establish control over disputed tracts of land, as reflected in a riot which occurred near Wolverhampton in 1850, when 500 Irish navvies employed, respectively, by the London and North-Western Railway and the Shrewsbury and Birmingham Railway fought a pitched battle, which was only ended by the deployment of police, armed with cutlasses, and troops, with bayonets fixed.[38] Such disorders were largely confined to the 1830s and 1840s. Moreover, they suggest, contrary to popular belief, that the Irish did not have a monopoly of navvy violence; indeed, about one third of navvies were Irish, one third English and one third Scottish and, because of this potentially combustible mixture, most navvy gangs were segregated.[39]

In contrast, inter-communal disorders which, on the surface at least, were rooted in religious differences between the Irish and the host society were frequently the product of violence directed against Irish Catholics, which often provoked a violent response. This was particularly evident during the mid-Victorian period, when the resurgence of popular Protestantism in the wake of the re-establishment of the Catholic hierarchy provided an additional cutting edge to Anglo-Irish tensions and contributed to a number of serious anti-Catholic and anti-Irish disorders, most notably at Stockport in 1852, when the homes of Irish Catholics in Rock Row were besieged by a Protestant mob and the Roman Catholic Church of Saints Philip and James was desecrated.[40] The activities of anti-Catholic lecturers such as Father Gavazzi, the Baron de Camin, and William Murphy also fomented communal violence. Murphy, a member of the Protestant Evangelical

Mission and Electoral Union, became the apostle of popular anti-Catholicism between 1867 and 1871 and his lectures sparked serious disorders in the Irish districts of many towns[41] until his premature death, as a result of injuries inflicted upon him by Irish miners as he prepared to address Whitehaven Orangemen in the Oddfellows Hall in 1871.

Thus variety was the hallmark of the disorders in which Irish migrants became embroiled, and many of these reflected purely local and regional tensions. Recent work on Anglo-Irish conflict in the towns and pit villages of Northumberland and Durham has pointed to numerous disturbances - sometimes instigated by the English, sometimes by the Irish - which resulted in eleven deaths and six capital convictions for murder between 1847 and 1877. Here, serious disorders in Durham, Newcastle, Shotley Bridge, Jarrow, Hebburn and Consett arose either from the activities of the Orange Order or from local economic factors, which fomented clashes between English and Irish workers, while the less serious disorders arose primarily from cultural differences, the Irish being considered different on account of accent, clothing, politics, and religion. Moreover, these disturbances also suggest that some of the factors that apparently contributed to Anglo-Irish conflict in other parts of England were largely absent in the North East. [42]

Yet the extent to which disorder invariably accompanied the Irish presence in the Victorian city remains problematic. Indeed, studies of the Irish experience in Coventry,[43] Chester[44] and Leicester[45] paint a different picture. In these towns, the relative absence of disturbances involving the Irish not only signifies a measured degree of accommodation into local society, but also reveals the divisions within the Irish community between those who engaged in fights and challenged the police and those who preferred to co-exist peacefully with their fellow countrymen and English neighbours. Similarly, a riot which occurred in Camborne, Cornwall, in 1882, does not fit easily into the general pattern of disorders involving the Irish. Here, the attack by Cornish tin miners on Irish Catholics was largely the product of a local popular tradition of protest against injustice by authority; in this case, the perception of a too lenient sentence imposed on two Irishmen for an assault on a Cornishman.[46] Studies such as these remind us that Victorian towns were far from monochrome and that, accordingly, the Irish urban experience was itself characterised by diversity in both time and place.

But why were the Irish poor generally over-represented in certain categories of criminal behaviour? In seeking to explain this, it is necessary to explore the bigger picture and to examine Irish criminality in several inter-related and mutually reinforcing contexts.

Firstly, any examination of Irish crime and disorder during the Victorian period needs to be placed in the broader context of English attitudes to the Irish, which have a complex history.[47] Although hostility to the Irish had ancient roots, the growth of anti-Hibernian sentiment during the early and mid-Victorian years was a consequence of the economic, social, political and religious currents of the period and was intimately linked to the scale of immigration from Ireland during the Famine,[48] which exacerbated hostility to the Irish poor by raising the profile of the contemporary social ills of poverty, public health and crime, for which the Irish emerged as convenient scapegoats.[49] English antipathy to the Catholic Irish was exacerbated by the restoration of the Catholic hierarchy in England and Wales in 1850 and, over the next twenty years, both public and government went through a phase of anti-Catholicism in response to "Papal aggression". Indeed, most anti-Irish disorders belong to this period, notably in South Lancashire,[50] where the situation was compounded by the activities of the Orange Order.[51] Political factors also fanned the flames of anti-Irish feeling, particularly between 1865 and 1868, when Fenian activities on the mainland brought a sense of fear of Irish nationalist violence to the host population. The dramatic events of 1867, which witnessed the abortive Fenian raid on Chester Castle, the case of the "Manchester Martyrs" and the Clerkenwell bombing, all served to raise Anglo-Irish tensions, albeit temporarily. The last-named incident - when a barrel of explosives, placed outside the wall of the exercise yard at Clerkenwell Gaol in an abortive attempt to release Fenian prisoners, exploded, killing twelve civilians and injuring 120 others - understandably resulted in popular outrage and panic, as embodied in John Tenniel's famous *Punch* cartoon, *The Fenian Guy Fawkes*, which not only condemned the Fenian dynamiter, but also played on old anti-Catholic prejudices by presenting it as a new version of the Gunpowder Plot.[52] It has also been argued that economic competition between English and Irish workers exacerbated native reactions to the newcomers, as the Irish threatened to undercut wage levels and were prepared to work as strike-breakers.[53] Thus, it might appear that poor working-class Irish Catholic immigrants were in some respects the "outcasts" of mid-Victorian society, on the grounds of their poverty, ethnicity, religion and politics, although in fact the Irish experience in the Victorian city was more diverse and complex than this imagery suggests, particularly during the late Victorian period.[54] Nevertheless, Irish nationalists claimed that the perceived association between the Irish, crime and disorder was only one manifestation of the sustained hostility, rooted in English prejudice, which was directed towards the Irish. Thus, in June 1868, *The Nation*, a Dublin weekly newspaper, observed that: "Nowhere in England can our countrymen consider themselves safe from English mob violence",[55] whilst in 1892 John Denvir noted: "We know how, by studied insults to his creed and country, the hot-blooded Irish Celt is often made to appear the aggressor".[56] More recently, this theme has been developed further by some historians, who have pointed not only to the over-representation of the Irish in the statistics of crime and disorder, but also to violence in the workplace, psychological terror, small-scale brawls, attacks on individuals and a routine diet of discrimination as the more usual means by which the non-Irish vented their aggressions on Irish migrants.[57] This may have been so, but of greater importance was the widely-held perception that Irish peasant society was inherently brutal, demonstrating a fundamental weakness of the Irish national character. The stereotype of the brutalised "Paddy" was entrenched in the public mind even before the Famine, and the subsequent experiences of the pauper Irish, who brought rural traditions with them and had yet to adapt to the mores of urban-industrial society, served only to reinforce these ingrained perceptions. Thus, Irish districts were *expected* to be hotbeds of crime, and anti-social behaviour by the Irish merely confirmed preconceived notions regarding the irresponsibility and criminality of the Celt.[58] It also, of course, influenced the attitudes of police and magistrates in their attempts to maintain law and order in urban Britain.

Secondly, Irish criminality in Victorian Britain also needs to be examined and understood in the context of patterns of crime in Ireland which, though fluctuating in time and place, were in some ways different from those of England and Wales during this period (although committals were increasing in both). With the exception of Dublin and Cork, crime was overwhelmingly rural, and convict records shed some light on the nature of Irish criminality. Approximately 160,000 convicts were transported to Australia between 1788 and 1868,[59] of whom roughly a quarter - 30,000 men and 9,000 women - came directly from Ireland, mostly for less serious offences such as petty theft and assault. A further 6,000 Irish convicts were transported from England, largely for crimes indistinguishable from those of ordinary British offenders.[60] But those transported from Ireland also included social and political protesters, who comprised 62% of all persons transported from Ireland and Britain for crimes of protest during the period: (i.e. 2,250 Irish out of a total of 3,604). Whilst a minority of these were political prisoners - United Irishmen, Young Irelanders, and Fenians - the majority were the representatives of various Irish agrarian movements who had sought to redress the grievances of the Irish peasantry by crimes of "outrage" - violent crimes against property, such as arson, armed robbery, forcible possession of property, armed assembly, attacks on houses and land, and assaults - all of which formed part of agrarian protest.[61]

Thus, to many contemporary observers, Irish peasant society appeared inherently lawless, violent and brutal. Faction fights provide one illustration of this. Observing the proceedings at Waterford Assizes in July 1835, Alexis de Tocqueville commented: "16 cases of murder. All these affairs turned out to be voluntary manslaughter or negligent homicide. But in all these affairs, I believe, a man had been killed. These assizes gave us the very clear impression that the lower classes of this county are very prone to quarrelling and fighting; that nearly every village forms a kind of faction, which has a soubriquet. Factions that began nobody knows when and continue nobody knows why, without taking on any political significance. When men of these different factions meet each other at a fair, a wedding, or elsewhere, it is rare they do not come to blows for the sole pleasure of the excitement that a fight gives. These quarrels very often end in the death of someone. In general a man's life here seems of very little value".[62] Indeed, faction fights proliferated in nineteenth-century Ireland[63] and sometimes involved large numbers: one such fight at a fair in Mallow in August 1821 (the Twomeys and Swineys against the Mahoneys) involved 500 on each side and resulted in many injuries.[64] Although the motives for faction fights varied, they could also be regarded as an illustration of violence as sport in nineteenth-century Ireland. Indeed, these fights were distinguished by clearly defined rules, willing participants, a sense of pleasure and an absence of malicious intent. The scale of faction fights was under-reported in the statistics of crime, because the parties were rarely arrested; even when serious injuries and fatalities resulted and warrants were issued, the parties were usually acquitted. Even in the case of brawls, which were characterised by the use of fists, feet, teeth, stones and even knives, severe punishment of offenders was unlikely, because there was usually an absence of malice.[65] Given the strength of the tradition of faction fighting in Ireland - which, in British eyes, provided further evidence of the inability of the Irish to govern themselves (thereby endorsing the value of the Union) – it is little wonder that this tradition was maintained by some Irish migrants in British cities during the nineteenth century. Indeed, given the violent nature of much crime in Ireland, it is somewhat surprising that Irish crime in Britain was not more violent than was actually the case.

Thus, the realties of Irish criminality were sometimes at odds with British perceptions. This theme was examined in an article published in the *Dublin Review* in 1857. The author, R. J. Gainsford, noted: "There are some people who live and die in the belief that everything Catholic is inferior to anything Protestant. They have always been told so, everybody says so, and of course it must be so ... on the particular subject of crime the phrase commonly adopted and circulated will be flavoured with Protestantism and love of country, two very acceptable ingredients, and thus of course become the reigning belief of general society ... and doubtless every English foolometer will repeat that the people in Catholic countries are far more criminal than in Protestant countries, and especially that Ireland is very black indeed when compared with England".[66] In seeking to challenge this thesis, Gainsford compared and contrasted the *Criminal Returns* for England and Wales with those for Ireland in 1854, noting that convictions (as opposed to committals) in England and Wales exceeded those in Ireland both in number (in proportion to the population) and in enormity of offence, and observing that: "Ireland is more addicted to crimes of personal violence and England to crimes of fraud or of violence arising from motives of lucre".[67] Gainsford's concluding remarks are interesting, if not entirely surprising: "These returns vindicate the character of poor and Catholic Ireland, when compared with rich and Protestant England; and we repeat that ... the convictions for crime, and especially for the more heinous crimes, are considerably less in proportion to the population in Ireland than in England and Wales. The greater poverty of Ireland would prepare us to expect a greater number of invasions upon property crimes; the contrary is the fact, and we cannot hesitate to attribute this fact to the influence of our holy Religion ... The lesson which these returns teach to Ireland is, that her character, though bearing on the whole an advantageous comparison with that of England and Wales, yet does not shine with that degree of superior brightness which would otherwise distinguish her, because so many of her sons are yet slaves to passion, and revenge, and drink, for to these causes, we presume, may be attributed the assaults and riots which form one sixth of all the crimes for which Irishmen are convicted. On the other hand, dishonesty and fraud, in all the forms in which they can develop themselves, seem peculiarly to preponderate in England and Wales".[68]

A third context concerns contemporary efforts to combat crime and disorder in British cities during the Victorian period and, in particular, the impact of developments in provincial policing. The practices of the "new police" forces that emerged in consequence of the Municipal Corporations Act of 1835, the County Police Act of 1839 and the County and Borough Police Act of 1856 represented an intrusion into working-class districts not previously kept under regular surveillance, and the targets of these provincial forces were, in essence, varieties of "street crime", which included drunkenness, disorderly behaviour, petty theft, vagrancy, and unruly forms of popular leisure and recreation.[69] Moreover, police forces were sometimes under considerable local pressure to achieve results in order to justify their expense. Since Irish migrants tended to live in the most intensively policed inner-city districts and were distinguished in the public mind by an unenviable reputation for the very offences that the police were directed to control, they were doubly vulnerable. Moreover, there is some evidence to suggest that the Irish districts of some towns were deliberately targeted by the police, which in part explains the high level of prosecutions of the Irish-born in specific criminal categories in towns such as Wolverhampton, Manchester, Birmingham, Bradford and Middlesbrough.[70] This raises the question of the extent to which the police were prejudiced against the Irish per se. It has been suggested, for example, that police prejudice was evident in Birmingham during the Murphy Riots of 1867. Here, the police did little to prevent the rioters' entry into the Irish quarter or the destruction and ransacking of Irish houses, yet a majority of those prosecuted after the riot bore Irish names and were charged with throwing stones at the police from *inside* their houses.[71] It is also possible that many assaults by the Irish on the police represented a response by the Irish to a perceived victimisation by the police, although it is important to acknowledge that an anti-police culture was prevalent among many Catholics and Protestants in Ireland before they migrated to Britain; hence clashes with British policemen in Victorian towns could be regarded in part as an extension of a traditional dislike of police authority in Ireland.[72] It is also possible that the deliberate policing of the Irish, as well as other outcast groups, enhanced police popularity in mainstream society. By creating scapegoats - the habitual criminal, the habitual drunkard, the disorderly Irish - Victorian anxieties were displaced and focused on the enemy within.[73] On the other hand, many policemen were themselves Irish: of 47 Chief Constables appointed between 1839 and 1880, 14 possessed previous experience in the Royal Irish Constabulary,[74] and there were significant numbers of Irish policemen - Catholic and Protestant - in some provincial forces, including Manchester.[75] Moreover, despite evidence of intensive policing in Irish districts in some towns, which was often counter-productive in that it fomented more serious clashes between the police and the Irish, many provincial policemen were afraid of executing their duties in volatile Irish districts without considerable support which, when provided, only fuelled Irish suspicions that they were being discriminated against. Police "prejudice", therefore, might perhaps be better explained in terms of a general discrimination against the "dangerous" or "criminal" sections of working-class society, within which the Irish were particularly vulnerable, rather than in terms of prejudice against the Irish per se. Of greater significance, perhaps, is the fact that more forms of behaviour were being criminalised during the Victorian period. By 1901, British males stood a one in twenty-four chance of being prosecuted for an indictable or non-indictable offence, and for both newcomers to city life and for young, single, unemployed, male slum-dwellers - among whom the Irish bulked large - the chances of a policeman's hand descending on your shoulders were several times higher.[76] Moreover, the over-representation of the Irish in committals to prison also requires further qualification and cannot be explained simply in terms of a general prejudice by provincial magistrates against the Irish when determining sentences. Indeed, it may well be that the petty offences for which the Irish were largely prosecuted carried a greater likelihood of successful detection and prosecution, making imprisonment a more likely scenario for those convicted, although further research on this subject is necessary before any conclusions may be drawn in support of either claim.

Finally, there is the context of Irish poverty, which many British Protestants ascribed to the deleterious effects of Roman Catholicism. Much Irish criminality was clearly the by-product of a poverty-ridden and brutalising urban slum environment, although even here it is important to acknowledge that many poor people, Irish and non-Irish, were law-abiding. As the Catholic newspaper, *The Tablet*, observed in 1846, "The fact is that there are two classes of Irish labouring people who differ about as widely as light and darkness - There are many who are industrious, methodical, orderly, thrifty and generous in the highest degree. But ask anyone to show you where 'the Irish' live. He will take you to a miserable cul-de-sac, which you are afraid of penetrating, and which, bad as it is physically, bears a moral character even worse. There are times when no policeman who is careful of his life dare show himself within that sacred enclosure".[77] Thus it was the worst-off Irish poor who were associated in the public mind with crime and disorder, and in a sense this mirrors the more negative attitudes of the period towards the poorest sections of the English working class.

The plight of Irish street children offers one illustration of this theme. It could well be that the disproportionate number of Irish children sent to prison during the mid-Victorian period is explained by the fact that the Irish lived more desperate lives than their neighbours and consequently had more reason to turn to crime,[78] although the extent to which the lives of the poorest Irish were any more desperate that those of the poorest non-Irish is problematic. The *Report on the State of the Irish Poor* noted the large number of Irish street children who were sent forth by their parents at an early age and instructed to steal,[79] an observation corroborated by many of the case-studies contained in the *Report of the Constabulary Commission* of 1839[80] and in the *Appendix to the Report from the Select Committee on Criminal and Destitute Juveniles* of 1852.[81] In 1849, the Chief Constable of Wolverhampton bemoaned the lack of recreational facilities for Irish street children in the town, with the result that "... they are to be found in different parts of the town, some begging and others thieving, whilst many of them become the associates of older persons, too well versed in crime, and are thus gradually led on to the commission of graver offences".[82] Henry Mayhew attributed Irish juvenile crime in London to the fact that "... the Irish constitute the poorest portion of our people, and the children, therefore, are virtually orphans in this country, left to gambol in the streets and courts, without parental control, from their very earliest years; the consequence is that the child grows up not only unacquainted with any industrial occupation, but untrained to habits of daily work; and long before he has learned to control the desire to appropriate the articles which he either wants or likes he has acquired furtive propensities from association with the young thieves located in his neighbourhood".[83] In similar vein, in 1861 the social reformer Mary Carpenter informed the Select Committee on the Education of Destitute Children that the Irish poor in Bristol were "… the very lowest class of population which can be found anywhere … the bulk of the families are known thieves; they keep in a gang together and in fact they rule the city, for the police dare not meddle with them". Yet she added that "… there are great capabilities in that class, some of the finest boys I know are Anglo-Irish".[84]

Vagrancy offers another illustration of the relationship between Irish poverty and crime. During the nineteenth century, vagrancy was a constant problem and vagrants were placed firmly within the category of the "dangerous classes".[85] The Constabulary Commission of 1839 argued that much crime was the product of migratory criminals in general and vagrants in particular, noting that many of the latter were Irish,[86] and although research has shed considerable doubt on the "migratory thesis",[87] it was nonetheless a powerful force behind contemporary perceptions of criminality, and the transience of Irish migrants made them particularly vulnerable to it. Although the stereotype of the Irish beggar was firmly fixed, much so-called "vagrancy" was in fact the seasonal movement of Irish harvesters and the migration of Irish navvies to new construction projects;[88] but the movement of thousands of poor Irish into British towns during the 1840s reinforced popular perceptions of the Irish vagrant as the carrier of crime and disease. The removal clauses of the Poor Law were invoked in ports of entry such as Cardiff and Liverpool in order to repatriate Irish paupers,[89] and the vagrancy laws were applied against Irish paupers in many towns, particularly for begging.⁹⁰ The Reverend John Clay, the Chaplain of Preston Gaol, reported in 1852 that twenty out of twenty-four Irish juveniles who had been imprisoned during the previous twelve months had been convicted of begging, although he acknowledged that they had been driven over to this country by the pressure of extreme want and were in a state of great wretchedness, adding that he knew of "... several exceptional cases in which Irish families have turned out the most industrious and in every way praiseworthy".⁹¹ It was perhaps unfortunate for Irish migrants in England that the Famine coincided with mounting public concern with the "Condition of England Question" and with the attempts of the provincial police to exercise their responsibilities, as assistant Poor Law officers, in regard to vagrants; in the industrial towns of South Wales, much police time was spent in searching, cautioning, arresting and registering vagrants, which was thus reflected in the criminal statistics.⁹² Yet, in reality, the actual scale of Irish vagrancy was generally at a lower level than contemporaries perceived it to be and allegations that that the Irish threw themselves disproportionately on local poor relief were based on prejudice rather than on fact. Moreover, public concern with the subject was in many respects transient, evaporating with the gradual decline in migration from Ireland towards the end of the century.⁹³

Thus we have some possible explanations for the over-representation of the Irish poor in the statistics of crime. Fundamental to these, however, were the problems of adaptation faced by newcomers to British society at a time of acute social and economic transformation and the social tensions arising from this process. Yet, as this lecture illustrates, much of the evidence pertaining to Irish criminality relates to the early and mid-Victorian years and is limited, selective and highly subjective, representing the views of the non-Irish and, in particular, those of the authorities, be they policemen, magistrates, prison officers, Poor Law guardians or clergymen. By contrast, we know relatively little of the relationship between Irish migration and crime during the late Victorian period and, until this subject is addressed by historians, it is difficult to assess how far the patterns of Irish criminality characteristic of the earlier period persisted into the 1880s, 1890s, and beyond. Quite simply, we do not know. This said, it does appear that from the 1870s onwards, public concern with Irish criminality in British cities was less transparent than it had been during the 1840s and 1850s, and in a sense this reflects the changing social, economic, political and cultural contexts of the late Victorian period, as well as the growing stability, consciousness and adaptability of Irish Catholic communities themselves. Moreover, the nature and pattern of urban crime, and attitudes towards it, were also changing during the period, and this had some bearing on the perceived link between the Irish and crime.

For example, the marked decline in the incidence of major disturbances involving the Irish - which, as we have seen, were often "anti-Irish" disorders - during the late Victorian period offers one illustration of change. The most serious disturbance occurred at Tredegar, South Wales, in July 1882, when economic rivalries between Irish and Welsh workers, exacerbated by the activities of local Salvationists and compounded by the anti-Irish feeling which had been aroused by the Phoenix Park murders in Dublin in May, resulted in several days of rioting, culminating in the eviction from the town of some 400 Irish men, women and children.[94] Any attempts to explain this decline should emphasise that relatively little is known about the Irish experience in late Victorian Britain, certainly in comparison with the more detailed and at times dramatic picture which emerges from the mid-

Victorian years.⁹⁵ Nevertheless, a number of possible explanations may be advanced. Firstly, the decline of disorders involving the Irish needs to be placed in the broader context of the general decline of violence and disorder and the emergence of a more orderly society during the late Victorian period, within which improved policing and improved techniques of riot control played their part.⁹⁶ Secondly, the decline in public disorder was a reflection of the changing face of protest in the context of the growth of more organised and institutional procedures for expressing working-class grievances, the impact of social reform, the extension of the franchise, and the distinctive cultural influences which shaped late Victorian society, including Irish migrants and their descendents.⁹⁷ Thirdly, it has been generally assumed that, just as the sudden increase in anti-Irish violence was a consequence of the Famine influx, coupled with mid-Victorian fears of Catholicism, so, with a subsequent decrease in Irish immigration, newcomers and hosts reached an accommodation, while the Catholic Church became less of a threat and more a part of the religious fabric of the nation. Thus, Irish immigration and its consequences were no longer contentious issues and the Irish were drawn into the institutions and social life of the areas in which they lived, although sectarian rivalries persisted in Merseyside and Clydeside.⁹⁸ Ironically, the perceived threat to society in the 1880s and 1890s came not from the Irish, but from the thousands of poor Jewish immigrants fleeing from persecution in Eastern Europe, who received a reception from the host society that was almost as hostile as that accorded to the pauper Irish in the 1840s.⁹⁹ Yet Jewish immigrants appear to have been have been far more quiescent and much more determined to keep to themselves than the Irish, although communal tensions sometimes ran high in those East London streets colonised by both Jewish and Irish migrants.[100] Finally, the tendency of the Irish, as a dynamic rather than a static group, to disperse within and between late Victorian towns and to integrate into urban society over time made them less visible and reduced their exposure to riots and other expressions of ethnic conflict, although anti-Irish sentiment may well have been expressed in more subtle and less public ways within working-class communities.[101]

Juvenile crime offers another useful illustration of this theme, for Irish youths contributed to the violent activities of neighbourhood-based street gangs in the working-class districts of late Victorian Manchester and Salford. These so-called "Scuttler" gangs, which comprised youths aged between 14 and 18, were variously armed and style-conscious, sporting a uniform of pointed clogs, bell-bottomed trousers cut off like a sailor's, and peaked caps, as well as distinctive haircuts, comprising a short back and sides with a long parted fringe at the front - all designed to indicate "hardness". Yet territory, rather than ethnic identity or religious affiliation, appears to have formed the basis of allegiance to these working-class gangs, for Irish Catholics and Irish Protestants shared the same loyalty to street and immediate neighbourhood and fought side by side in conflicts between local gangs.[102] The childhood experiences of Pat O'Mara in the Grenville, Cornwallis and Parr Streets district of Edwardian Liverpool reveal a similar picture, for O'Mara's juvenile gang included, in addition to Irish Catholics, three Protestants, an Italian, a Spaniard and a German.[103]

These examples clearly provide food for thought, but they also point to an agenda for further research on Irish criminality during the late Victorian period and beyond. Systematic studies of the statistics of Irish crime on national, regional and local levels are required, if further light is to be shed on the precise relationship between Irish migration, settlement and urban crime.[104] The relationship between Irish women and crime - a vastly under-researched subject - is certainly worthy of attention.[105] Did Irish women continue, as in the industrial towns of South Wales,[106] to be over-represented in prosecutions for assault, disorderly behaviour, petty theft and vagrancy? Did they figure disproportionately in offences arising from prostitution, as was sometimes alleged?[107] In both cases, the picture is misty and points to the need for further scholarly enquiry. Irish involvement in domestic violence is another under-researched area. There is some evidence, for example, that the Irish-born figured disproportionately in prosecutions for intimate homicide (of female spouses, in particular) between 1835 and 1905,[108] which of course also opens up the whole question of how far the Irish-born were over-represented in prosecutions for certain other categories of serious crime, which also warrants further scrutiny. Finally, there is a need to place Irish crime in urban Britain in a wider comparative context, by reference to Irish criminality in the countries of the Irish Diaspora, most notably the USA and Australia, where substantial research on this subject has been undertaken.[109]

In short, much remains to be achieved by historians if we are to assess adequately the extent to which Irish men and women were guilty of "behaving badly" in the Victorian city. If "behaving badly" is defined simply in terms of committing an action which violates the criminal law at a specific time and suffering the consequences, the answer, on the evidence to date, is both "Yes" and "No". Some Irish migrants did break the law, and for some of the reasons explored in this paper; yet so too did many more English, Scottish and Welsh people. By contrast, countless Irish men, women and juveniles were essentially law-abiding and faced the day-to-day difficulties and uncertainties of life in the Victorian city without coming into formal contact with policemen, magistrates and prison officers. Nevertheless, the study of the relationship between Irish migrants and crime is important. Firstly, it offers insights into contemporary attitudes to "the other" in Victorian society. The very presence of the Irish poor in British cities enabled contemporary tensions in society to be deflected on to external factors, thereby helping to define English, or Welsh, or Scottish identities,[110] while the particular emphasis on the capacity of the Irish for breaking the law served also to highlight in British eyes the relative orderliness of the non-Irish (which was little more than a myth).[111] Secondly, it provides a window on the complex and diverse experience of Irish migrants, and attitudes towards them, in Victorian Britain, not least in terms of their relationship with the police and the criminal justice system. In a sense, that experience, influenced as it was by issues of identity, community and nationality, and involving processes of alienation, regulation, adaptation and accommodation, provides an historical exemplar which is not without relevance to the study of immigrants and minorities in a pluralist society today. Thirdly, it serves to remind us of some of the continuities in the public debate on crime and crime prevention in modern British society. There has always been an Irish thread within this debate and a continuing dialogue between past and present, most notably in regard to irreversible developments in policing practice, where Ireland and the Irish have provided a training ground for innovation, albeit in the specific context of politically-motivated crime. Here, the thread extends from Peel's experiments with policing arrangements in Ireland in the years before the Metropolitan Police Act of 1829 was applied in England, and the establishment in 1884 of the Special Branch (originally designated the Special *Irish* Branch) to deal with Irish-American bomb-planters, to the deployment of rubber bullets in Ulster during the "Troubles".[112] But that is another story.

Notes

[1] For further details, see especially James Handley, *The Irish in Scotland, 1798-1845* (Cork: Cork University Press, 1943); James Handley, *The Irish in Modern Scotland* (Cork: Cork University Press; Oxford: Basil Blackwell, 1947); John Archer Jackson, *The Irish in Britain* (London: Routledge & Kegan Paul, 1963); *The Irish in the Victorian City*, ed. by Roger Swift & Sheridan Gilley (London: Croom Helm, 1985); *The Irish in Britain, 1815-1939*, ed. by Roger Swift & Sheridan Gilley (London: Pinter, 1989); Graham Davis, *The Irish in Britain, 1815-1914* (Dublin: Gill and Macmillan, 1990); Frank Neal, *Black '47: Britain and the Famine Irish* (Basingstoke: Macmillan, 1997); Donald MacRaild, *Irish Migrants in Modern Britain, 1750-1922* (Basingstoke: Macmillan, 1999); *The Irish in Victorian Britain: The Local Dimension*, ed. by Roger Swift & Sheridan Gilley (Dublin: Four Courts Press, 1999); Paul O'Leary, *Immigration and Integration: The Irish in Wales, 1798-1922* (Cardiff: University of Wales Press, 2000).

[2] *Report on the State of the Irish Poor in Great Britain.* Parliamentary Papers (London: 1836), [40], xxxiv, pp. 20-23.

[3] *Report of the Royal Commission to Inquire into the Best Means of Establishing an Efficient Constabulary Force in the Counties of England and Wales.* Parliamentary Papers (London: 1839), [169], xix, p. 89, s.97.

[4] Thomas Carlyle, *Chartism,* Everyman's Library (London: Dent, 1972; original ed., 1839), pp. 182-183.

⁵ Revd. Joseph Dare, *Ninth Report of the Leicester Domestic Mission Society* (Leicester: 1854), pp. 10-11.

⁶ See Flora Tristan, *Promenades dans Londres* (Paris: H.-L. Delloye, 1840), pp. 134-35: Observing the Irish in St. Giles, London, she noted that " ... all of them, men and women alike, live off thievery; and old people beg", adding " ... if I had seen this district before Newgate I would not have been surprised to learn that fifty to sixty children are sent there every month"; see also Leon Faucher, *Manchester in 1844: Its Present Condition and Future Prospects* (London: Simpkin, Marshall and Co., 1844), p. 28: Faucher noted that the Irish in Manchester were " ... perpetually in a state of agitation".

⁷ See, for example, Frances Finnegan, *Poverty and Prejudice: A Study of Irish Migrants in York, 1840-75* (Cork: Cork University Press, 1982), pp. 132-54; William J. Lowe, 'The Irish in Lancashire, 1846-71', (unpublished doctoral thesis, Trinity College, Dublin, 1975); Clem Richardson, 'The Irish in Victorian Bradford', *The Bradford Antiquary,* 9 (1976), 311; Roger Swift, 'Another Stafford Street Row: Law, Order and the Irish Presence in Mid-Victorian Wolverhampton', *Immigrants & Minorities,* 3 (1984), 5-29; Helen Peavitt, 'The Irish, Crime and Disorder in Chester, 1841-1871', (unpublished doctoral thesis, University of Liverpool, 2000); D. Taylor, 'Policing and the Community: Late Twentieth-century Myths and Late Nineteenth-century Realities', in *Social Conditions, Status and Community, 1860-1920,* ed. by Keith Laybourn (Stroud: Sutton, 1997), pp. 104-22.

⁸ *Report on the State of the Irish Poor*, pp. 40-41.

⁹ Frank Neal, *Sectarian Violence: The Liverpool Experience,*

1819-1914 (Manchester: Manchester University Press, 1988), pp. 110-15.

[10] *Judicial Statistics, England and Wales, 1861-1901*. House of Commons Papers (London: [1901]), 16. The Irish comprised 15% of all committals in 1861 (an index of over-representation of 4.9), 14% in 1871 (5.7), 12% in 1881 (5.7), 8% in 1891 (5.3), and 7% in 1901 (5.6).

[11] For example, in Carlisle Gaol in 1861, 23.4% males were Irish-born, 12.6% female; in 1871 18.9% males were Irish-born, 16.6% female: see MacRaild, *Irish Migrants in Modern Britain*, p. 163.

[12] Peavitt, p. 182.

[13] *Chester Chronicle*, 2 January 1869, 9 January 1869, 13 February 1869, 3 July 1869; Chester City Gaol, *Matron's Daily Report Book*, 4 February 1870.

[14] P. J. Waller, *Democracy and Sectarianism: A Political and Social History of Liverpool, 1868-1939* (Liverpool: Liverpool University Press, 1981), p. 25.

[15] *Report on the State of the Irish Poor*, p. 19.

[16] *Report on the State of the Irish Poor*, pp. 19-20, 57. William Parlour, the Superintendent of the Liverpool Police reported that "... there are perhaps from four to six cases of manslaughter among the Irish in a year; deliberate murders are very rare among them", whilst Michael Whitty, the Superintendent of the Liverpool Night Watch, observed that "... as to crimes against property, few robbers or regular thieves are Irish". The Rev. Daniel Hearn made similar observations of the Manchester Irish,

noting that, although drunken rows often led to assaults and sometimes manslaughter, "... there is not much legal crime among the Irish of my flock; nor is there much pilfering". Similarly, Gilbert Hogg, the Chief Constable of Wolverhampton, reported in 1849 that the majority of commitments from the Irish quarter "... are mainly for offences against the public peace, and not for the crime of felony; the number of commitments of that kind being comparatively few": *Report to the Board of Health on the Sanitary Condition of Wolverhampton,* Parliamentary Papers (London: 1849), (292), pp. 28-9.

[17] See David Jones, *Crime, Protest, Community and Police in Nineteenth Century Britain* (London: Routledge & Kegan Paul, 1982), pp. 117-43; Tom Dillon, 'The Irish in Leeds, 1851-61', *Thoresby Miscellany,* 16 (1979), 1-29; Finnegan, pp. 132-54.

[18] Roger Swift, 'Crime and the Irish in Nineteenth Century Britain', in *The Irish in Britain, 1815-1939* (see Swift & Gilley, above), pp. 163-82; see also Roger Swift, 'Heroes or Villains?: The Irish, Crime and Disorder in Victorian England', *Albion,* 29, 3 (1997), 399-421.

[19] Brian Harrison, *Drink and the Victorians: The Temperance Question in England, 1815-1822* (Keele: Keele University Press, 1994; original ed., 1971), pp. 156-58.

[20] *Third Report of the Select Committee on Intemperance.* Parliamentary Papers (London: 1877), (418), xi, p. 159, s.5158.

[21] John Denvir, *The Irish in Britain: from the Earliest Times to the Fall and Death of Parnell* (London: Kegan Paul, Trench, Trubner, 1892), p. 253.

[22] The Chief Constable of Wolverhampton observed in 1849 that "… many are tempted to spend their time and money in these places from the total want of comfort at their own houses; indeed, many of them have told me, after having been turned out of the public house, that the place in which they lived was in such a miserable state that they would rather remain out in the open air if the weather was not severe": *Report on the Sanitary Condition of Wolverhampton,* pp. 28-9.

[23] *Report of the Select Committee on Public Houses.* Parliamentary Papers (London: 1852-3), (292), xxxvii.

[24] *Report on the State of the Irish Poor,* appendix I, pp. 40-41.

[25] MacRaild, *Irish Migrants in Modern Britain,* p. 164; see also J. R. Barrett, 'Why Paddy drank: the social importance of whiskey in pre-Famine Ireland', *Journal of Popular Culture,* 11 (1977).

[26] Elizabeth Malcolm, *"Ireland Sober, Ireland Free": Drink and Temperance in Nineteenth Century Ireland* (Dublin: Gill and Macmillan, 1986), pp. 329-34.

[27] Harrison, pp. 155-58.

[28] W. J. Lowe, *The Irish in Mid-Victorian Lancashire* (New York: Peter Lang, 1989), pp. 217-18.

[29] *Report on the State of the Irish Poor,* p. 23.

[30] For further details of the growth of the Orange Order, see especially Hereward Senior, *Orangeism in Ireland and Britain, 1795-1835* (London: Routledge & Kegan Paul,

1966), and Elaine McFarland, *Protestants First: Orangeism in Nineteenth Century Scotland* (Edinburgh: Edinburgh University Press, 1990). For Liverpool, see Waller; Tom Gallagher, 'A Tale of Two Cities: Communal Strife in Glasgow and Liverpool before 1914', in *The Irish in the Victorian City* (see Swift & Gilley, above), pp. 106-29; Neal, *Sectarian Violence*; and the essays by Anne Bryson, 'Riotous Liverpool, 1815-60', and John Bohstedt, 'More than One Working Class: Protestant and Catholic Riots in Edwardian Liverpool', in *Popular Politics, Riot and Labour: Essays in Liverpool History, 1790-1940*, ed. by John Belchem (Liverpool: Liverpool University Press, 1992), pp. 98-134, 173-216. For Glasgow, see Tom Gallagher, *Glasgow, the Uneasy Peace: Religious Tension in Modern Scotland* (Manchester: Manchester University Press, 1987).

[31] *Glasgow Herald*, 13 July 1857.

[32] For further details, see Donald MacRaild, *Culture, Conflict and Migration: the Irish in Victorian Cumbria* (Liverpool: Liverpool University Press, 1998).

[33] *Report of the Royal Commission [on the] Constabulary Commission,* pp. 87-8.

[34] *Report on the Sanitary Condition of Wolverhampton*, p. 28.

[35] Lowe, *The Irish in Mid-Victorian Lancashire*, p. 102.

[36] Barbara Weinburger, 'The Police and the Public in Mid-Nineteenth Century Warwickshire', in *Policing and Punishment in Nineteenth-Century Britain,* ed. by Victor Bailey (London: Croom Helm, 1982), pp. 69-71.

[37] Terry Coleman, *The Railway Navvies* (London:

Hutchinson, 1965), pp. 83-90. These include a pitched battle between navvies working on the North Union Railway near Preston in 1838, as a result of which Preston Council reviewed policing arrangement in the town; three days of fierce fighting between 300 Irish navvies and 250 English railway labourers engaged on the line of the Chester and Birkenhead Railway at Childer Thornton in 1839, which was only ended by the use of troops from Chester and Liverpool; and the serious clashes between English and Irish navvies on the Lancaster and Carlisle line at Penrith and Kendal in 1846.

[38] Swift, 'Another Stafford Street Row', 5-29.

[39] Coleman, p. 84.

[40] See especially Pauline Millward, 'The Stockport Riots of 1852: A Study of anti-Catholic and anti-Irish sentiment', in *The Irish in the Victorian City* (see Swift & Gilley, above), pp. 207-224. These disorders offer a useful illustration of the extent to which the inter-play of a variety of factors influenced violence against the Irish. For example, the riots may have arisen from the underlying antagonism between Irish immigrants and the hard-pressed English cotton workers who resented the incursion of cheap Irish labour into the mills, although this in itself was insufficient to cause the initial violence, the actual occasion being the restoration of the Catholic hierarchy, fanned to a flame by local Anglican clergymen and electorally vulnerable Tory politicians, who played the Irish card in a bid for political power.

[41] These included Wolverhampton, Rochdale, Ashton, Oldham, Bury, Blackburn, Hanley, Stalybridge, Tynemouth, and Whitehaven. For further details, see

especially: Walter Arnstein, 'The Murphy Riots: A Victorian Dilemma', *Victorian Studies*, 19 (1975), 55-71; Donald Richter, *Riotous Victorians* (Athens: Ohio University Press, 1981), pp. 35-50; Roger Swift, 'Anti-Catholicism and Irish Disturbances: Public Order in Mid-Victorian Wolverhampton', *Midland History*, 9 (1984), 87-108; Donald MacRaild, 'William Murphy, the Orange Order and Communal Violence: the Irish in West Cumberland, 1871-84', in *Racial Violence in Britain, 1840-1950*, ed. by Panikos Panayi (Leicester: Leicester University Press, 1993), pp. 44-64.

[42] Frank Neal, 'English-Irish Conflict in the North-East of England', in *The Irish in British Labour History*, ed. by Patrick Buckland & John Belchem (Liverpool: Institute of Irish Studies, University of Liverpool, 1993), pp. 59-85. Neal argues that some of the factors that apparently contributed to Anglo-Irish conflict in other parts of England were largely absent in the North-East, in that the regional economy, based on coal, iron, and shipbuilding, expanded during the period and there is no evidence that the Irish affected adversely real wages; the scale of Irish immigration just was not big enough; the vitriolic anti-Catholicism of South Lancashire was almost totally absent; and press concern over the alleged financial burden of the Irish poor was relatively muted.

[43] Paul Mulkern, 'Irish Immigrants and Public Disorder in Coventry, 1845-1875', *Midland History*, 21 (1996), 119-35.

[44] Kristina Jeffes, 'The Irish in Early Victorian Chester: An Outcast Community?', in *Victorian Chester: Essays in Social History, 1830-1900*, ed. by Roger Swift (Liverpool: Liverpool University Press, 1996), pp. 85-118; Peavitt, pp.

256-63.

[45] Nessan Danaher, 'The Irish in Leicester, 1841-1881: A Study of a Minority Community in the East Midlands', (unpublished doctoral thesis, University of North London, 2000), pp. 389-94, 462-70.

[46] Louise Miskell, 'Irish Immigrants in Cornwall: the Camborne Experience, 1861-1882', in *The Irish in Victorian Britain* (see Swift & Gilley, above), pp. 31-51.

[47] Sheridan Gilley, 'English Attitudes to the Irish in England, 1780-1900', in *Immigrants and Minorities in British Society*, ed. by Colin Holmes (London: Allen & Unwin, 1978), pp. 81-110.

[48] Alan O'Day, 'Varieties of Anti-Irish Behaviour in Britain, 1846-1922', in *Racial Violence in Britain, 1840-1950* (see Panayi, above), pp. 26-43; Roger Swift, "Anti-Irish Violence in Victorian England: Some Perspectives," *Criminal Justice History*, 15 (1994), 127-40.

[49] Graham Davis, 'Little Irelands', in *The Irish in Britain, 1815-1939* (see Swift & Gilley, above), pp. 104-33.

[50] See, for example, Neville Kirk, 'Ethnicity, Class and Popular Toryism, 1850-1870', in *Hosts, Immigrants and Minorities*, ed. by Kenneth Lunn (Folkestone: Dawson, 1980), pp. 64-106.

[51] See, for example, Gallagher, 'A Tale of Two Cities', pp. 106-29; Neal, *Sectarian Violence*, pp. 37-79, 151-175; Frank Neal, 'Manchester Origins of the English Orange Order', *Manchester Region History Review*, (1990), 12-24.

[52] William J. Lowe, 'Lancashire Fenianism, 1864-71', *Transactions of the Historic Society of Lancashire and Cheshire*, 121 (1977), 156-185; Patrick Quinlivan & Paul Rose, *The Fenians in England, 1865-72* (London: Calder, 1982), pp. 43-94; *Defining the Victorian Nation: Class, Race, Gender and the Reform Act of 1867*, ed. by Catherine Hall, Keith McClelland & Jane Rendall (Cambridge: Cambridge University Press, 2000), pp. 204-20.

[53] Arthur Redford, *Labour Migration in England, 1800-1850* (Manchester: Manchester University Press, 1964; original ed., 1926), pp. 159-164. However, there is some evidence to suggest that the Irish impact on wage rates has been exaggerated and that competition between English and Irish workers was essentially a product of the pre-Famine period; that there was relative harmony and some political and trades unionist co-operation between English and Irish workers; and that Irish and English cotton operatives sometimes acted in unison during moments of industrial militancy; see, for example, Jeffrey Williamson, 'The Impact of the Irish on British Labour Markets during the Industrial Revolution', *Journal of Economic History*, 46 (1986), 693-721; Edward Thompson, *The Making of the English Working Class* (London: Gollancz, 1963), pp. 469-485; John Foster, *Class Struggle and the Industrial Revolution* (London: Weidenfeld and Nicolson, 1974), p. 333; Kirk, pp. 64-106.

[54] *The Irish in the Victorian City* (see Swift & Gilley, above), pp. 1-12; see also Brenda Collins, 'The Irish in Britain, 1780-1921', in *An Historical Geography of Ireland*, ed. by B. J. Graham & L. J. Proudfoot (London: Academic Press, 1993), pp. 366-98.

[55] *The Nation*, 6 June 1868.

[56] Denvir, pp. 157-59, 460-62.

[57] O'Day, p. 26.

[58] Finnegan, p. 153.

[59] For further details, see especially Robert Hughes, *The Fatal Shore: A History of the Transportation of Convicts to Australia, 1878-1868* (London: Collins Harvill, 1987).

[60] A. G. L. Shaw, *Convicts and the Colonies: A Study of Penal Transportation from Great Britain and Ireland to Australia and Other Parts of the British Empire* (London: Faber, 1966), pp. 166-83.

[61] George Rudé, *Protest and Punishment: The Story of the Social and Political Protesters Transported to Australia, 1788-1868* (Oxford: Clarendon Press, 1978), pp. 8-10, 27-41, 103-12.

[62] *Alexis de Tocqueville's Journey in Ireland, July-August 1835*, ed. by Emmet Larkin (Dublin: Wolfhound, 1990), p. 53.

[63] See *Irish Peasants: Violence and Political Unrest, 1780-1914*, ed. by Samuel Clarke and James S. Donnelly, Jr. (Manchester: Manchester University Press, 1983); Gary Owens, 'A Moral Insurrection': Faction Fighters, Public Demonstrations and the O'Connellite Campaign, 1928', *Irish Historical Studies*, 30 (1997), 513-39.

[64] Donal McCartney, *The Dawning of Democracy: Ireland 1800-1870* (Dublin: Helicon, 1987), pp. 63-109.

[65] Carolyn Conley, 'The Agreeable Reaction of Fighting', *Journal of Social History*, 33 (1999), 57-72.

[66] R. J. Gainsford, 'English and Irish Crime', *Dublin Review*, 42 (1857), 142-3.

[67] Gainsford, 151.

[68] Gainsford, 156.

[69] See, for example, Robert D. Storch, 'The Plague of the Blue Locusts: Police Reform and Popular Resistance in Northern England, 1840-57', *International Review of Social History*, 20 (1975), 61-90.

[70] Roger Swift, 'Crime and Ethnicity: The Irish in Early Victorian Wolverhampton', *West Midlands Studies*, 13 (1980), 1-5; Jones, *Crime, Protest, Community and Police,* pp. 85-116; D. Taylor, *The New Police in Nineteenth-Century England: Crime, Conflict and Control* (Manchester: Manchester University Press, 1997), p. 123.

[71] Weinburger, pp. 69-71.

[72] See especially, Brian Griffin, *The Bulkies: Police and Crime in Belfast, 1800-1865* (Dublin: Irish Academic Press, 1997).

[73] Taylor, 'Policing and the Community', pp. 104-122.

[74] Carolyn Steedman, *Policing the Victorian Community* (London: Routledge and Kegan Paul, 1984), p. 48.

[75] Stephen Davies, 'Classes and Police in Manchester, 1829-1880', in *City, Class and Culture: Studies of Cultural Production and Social Policy in Victorian Manchester*, ed. by Alan Kidd & Kenneth Roberts (Manchester: Manchester

University Press, 1985), p. 34. Of 275 Irish policemen recruited between 1858 and 1869, a slight majority (148, or 54%) were Protestants.

[76] V. A. C. Gatrell, 'The Victorian State: Order or Liberty?', in *The Making of Britain: The Age of Revolution,* ed. by Lesley M. Smith (Basingstoke: Macmillan Education, 1987), pp. 89-102.

[77] *The Tablet,* 24 January 1846.

[78] John A. Stack, 'Children, Urbanization, and the Chances of Imprisonment in Mid-Victorian England', *Criminal Justice History*, 13 (1992), 133.

[79] *Report on the State of the Irish Poor*, Appendix II, pp. 19-20. William Parlour, the Liverpool Superintendent of Police, noted "… there is a great deal of pilfering among the Irish; many Irish women send children out to steal, and maintain them for the purpose of thieving".

[80] *Report of the Royal Commission [on the] Constabulary Commission,* p. 18, s.27. A prisoner in Salford Gaol observed in 1839 that "… they say that Manchester and Birmingham turn out more thieves than London and Liverpool; the Manchester and Liverpool are reckoned the most expert, they are thought to be of Irish parents and to have most cunning".

[81] *Report of the Select Committee on Criminal and Destitute Juveniles,* Parliamentary Papers (London, 1852), (515), vii, Appendix, pp. 393-402.

[82] *Report on the Sanitary Condition of Wolverhampton*, p. 30.

[83] Henry Mayhew & John Binny, *The Criminal Prisons of London, and Scenes of Prison Life* (London: Griffin, Bohn, 1862), pp. 402-03.

[84] *Report of the Select Committee on the Education of Destitute Children.* Parliamentary Papers (London, 1861), (460), vii, p. 95.

[85] For the classic study of the relationship between vagrancy and crime, see Jones, 'The Vagrant and Crime in Victorian Britain: Problems of Definition and Attitude', in *Crime, Protest, Community and Police,* pp. 178-209.

[86] *Report of the Royal Commission [on the] Constabulary Commission*, p. 67. It was noted of migratory criminals that "… three parts of those who are travelling now throughout the kingdom have Irish blood in them, either from father, mother, or grandmother".

[87] See, for example, Jenifer Hart, 'The Reform of the Borough Police, 1835-56', *English Historical Review*, 120 (1955), 411-27; Clive Emsley, *Crime and Society in England 1750-1900* (London: Longman, 1987), pp. 48-77; Roger Swift, 'Urban Policing in Early Victorian England, 1835-56: A Reappraisal', *History,* 73 (1988), 211-237.

[88] Lionel Rose, *'Rogues and Vagabonds': Vagrant Underworld in Britain, 1815-1985* (London: Routledge and Kegan Paul, 1988), pp. 6-7.

[89] For further details, see especially Neal, *Black '47.*

[90] Graham Davis has shown how the *Bath Chronicle* gleefully reported Irish vagrancy cases between 1847 and 1852. In Bath, it was local policy to despatch vagrants from

the city rather than to prosecute them; thus it was reported, for example, that "John Williams, an Irishman and his wife, destitute and two children, applied to the Police Station for relief. On being searched, a bottle of whiskey and 10d. found on them .... He was discharged with a caution to leave the city immediately", (Graham Davis, *Bath Beyond the Guide Book: Scenes from Victorian Life* [Bristol: Redcliffe, 1988], p. 13). By contrast, the authorities in York adopted a harsher policy towards Irish vagrants. In October 1848, the *Yorkshire Gazette* claimed that "… there is no doubt that our gaols obtain a large amount of their inmates from the class of vagrant children who infest our streets" (*Yorkshire Gazette,* 21 October 1848). In August 1849, when it was estimated that there were over 1,000 vagrants in the largely-Irish Bedern district, the York Watch Committee requested the city magistrates to impose harsher sentences for vagrancy, which the *York Herald* defined as "… nearly akin to theft" (*York Herald,* 11 August 1849).

[91] *Report of the Select Committee on Criminal and Destitute Juveniles,* p. 197, s.1695-7.

[92] David Jones, *Crime in Nineteenth-Century Wales* (Cardiff: University of Wales Press, 1992), pp. 161-64, 193-96.

[93] Jones, *Crime, Protest, Community and Police,* p. 183.

[94] Jon Parry, 'The Tredegar Anti-Irish Riots of 1882', *Llafur,* 3 (1983), 20-23; see also Denvir, pp. 294-312.

[95] Roger Swift, 'The Historiography of the Irish in Nineteenth-Century Britain', in *The Irish World Wide, Vol.2: The Irish in the New Communities,* ed. by Patrick O'Sullivan (Leicester: Leicester University Press, 1992), pp. 52-81.

[96] John Stevenson, *Popular Disturbances in England, 1700-1870* (London: Longman, 1979), pp. 316-23; Clive Emsley, *Policing and its Context, 1750-1870* (London: Macmillan, 1983), pp. 132-147.

[97] Swift, 'Anti-Irish Violence in Victorian England', 127-41.

[98] O'Day, p. 37.

[99] See, for example, Chaim Bermant, *London's East End: Point of Arrival* (London: Eyre Methuen, 1974), pp. 138-163; James Walvin, *Passage to Britain: Immigration in British History and Politics* (Harmondsworth: Penguin, 1984), pp. 61-75; Colin Holmes, *John Bull's Island: Immigration and British Society, 1871-1971* (Basingstoke: Macmillan, 1988), pp. 56-83; Vivian Lipman, *A History of the Jews in Britain since 1858* (Leicester: Leicester University Press, 1990), pp. 43-88.

[100] David Englander, 'Booth's Jews: The Presentation of Jews and Judaism in *Life and Labour of the People in London*', *Victorian Studies*, 32 (1988-89), 551-71.

[101] O'Day, p. 40.

[102] Andrew Davies, 'Youth Gangs, Masculinity and Violence in Late Victorian Manchester and Salford', *Journal of Social History* (1998), 349-69. For an illustration of later Irish involvement in the activities of Gorbals-based gangs in Glasgow, see Andrew Davies, 'Street Gangs, Crime and Policing in Glasgow during the 1930s: the case of the Beehive Boys', *Journal of Social History*, 23, 3 (1998), 251-67.

[103] Pat O'Mara, *The Autobiography of a Liverpool Irish Slummy* (London: Martin Hopkinson, 1934), Chapter 10, pp. 56-8.

O'Mara, who described himself as a "slummy Irish-Catholic Britisher", recalled: "Among the active members of our gang were Joe Manassi, a belligerent, stocky boy of Italian parentage; Harold May, Protestant, very English and quiet; Johnny Mangan, heavy set, Irish, belligerent; Johnny Ford, the same; Henry Roche, wiry, belligerent, Irish but no relation to me; my cousin Bernard Roche, thin, quiet, a true fighter; Frankie Roza, half-caste Protestant Manilla boy, who played the concertina and was the favourite of the gang; Jackie (Quanito) Sanchez, fiery yet amiable Spanish boy, whose mother kept the big Spanish boarding house at the corner of Cornwallis Street and Park Lane; 'Lepsey' Phillips, Protestant boy - mother, a very belligerent gypsy, and father, Irish - a quick tempered boy; Jackie Oldham, dare-devil and English; Freddie Seegar, comedian, of German-Irish parents, lazy and improvident; and a waif known to us all only as 'Mickey', an upcountry boy who had drifted into Liverpool and slept at the Working Boys' Home. The three Protestant members (Protestant only at the insistence of their parents) attended St Michael's Protestant School in Pitt Street. This was our 'gang' and our 'corner' was the empty house in White Street at Pitt, opposite Mrs Mallin's pub, until Aeroplane Joe, the bobby who wouldn't let us play pitch and toss, the war and death broke us up".

[104] Roger Swift, 'The Historiography of the Irish in Nineteenth-Century Britain: Some Perspectives', in *The Irish in British Labour History* (see Buckland & Belchem, above), pp. 11-18.

[105] See especially, Martha Kanya-Forstner, 'Defining Womanhood: Irish Women and the Catholic Church in Victorian Liverpool', in *The Great Famine and Beyond: Irish*

Migrants in Britain in the Nineteenth and Twentieth Centuries, ed. by Donald MacRaild (Dublin: Irish Academic Press, 2000), pp. 168-188.

[106] O'Leary, pp. 169-71.

[107] For the view that Irish-born women were drawn disproportionately into prostitution, see, for example, Montague Gore's description of the Irish in St Giles in 1851: "We believe that female profligacy is more rare in Ireland than in England, though poverty is more excessive, but the Irish coming to London seem to regard it as a heathen city and to give themselves up at once to a course of recklessness and crime. The purity of the female character which is the boast of Irish historians here at least is a fable", (Montague Gore, *On the Dwellings of the Poor and the Means of Improving Them* [London: J. Ridgway, 1851], pp. 12-14). This was disputed by Henry Mayhew, who remarked on the chastity of Irish women in London, in contrast with English street-sellers: "With the Irish girls the case is different; brought up to a street life, used to whine and blarney, they grow up to womanhood in street-selling, and as they rarely form impure connections, and as no-one may be induced to offer them marriage, their life is often one of street-celibacy", (Henry Mayhew, *London Labour and the London Poor* [London: Griffin, Bohn, 1851], I, pp. 448). There is evidence of a high proportion of Irish-born women among Liverpool's prostitutes: see Neal, 'A Criminal Profile of the Liverpool Irish', *Transactions of the Historic Society of Lancashire and Cheshire*, 40 (1990), 161-99. However, little research has been conducted on this subject in other Victorian towns, and it may be that the Liverpool experience was atypical. For example, a detailed analysis of prostitution in York between 1840 and 1875 concludes

that "... though poor, and concentrated in the main brothel area in the city, the immigrants contributed little to York's prostitution", for only 23 Irish girls were among the 619 prostitutes named in the Poor Law records and newspaper reports during the period (i.e., 3.7%; thus, the Irish were under-represented in this category) and the York press, though anti-Irish in tone, never accused the Irish of this particular vice: see Finnegan, pp. 134-143.

[108] I am indebted to Professor Martin Wiener for this information. By reference to the *Judicial Statistics* for England and Wales, police reports, contemporary newspapers, and confidential Home Office files pertaining to capital cases, Wiener has identified 1,050 convictions for domestic homicide during the period, noting that the Irish were represented disproportionately (at least 10% of the whole) within this number: M. Wiener, 'Intimate Homicide in Nineteenth-Century England', unpublished paper presented at a seminar on 'Crime and Violence in Nineteenth-Century England', University of Keele, July 1999.

[109] See, for example, Donald H. Akenson, *The Irish Diaspora: A Primer* (Toronto: P. D. Meany; Belfast: Institute of Irish Studies, Queen's University, 1996; original ed., 1993), pp. 118-19, 181-82.

[110] O'Leary, pp. 184-85.

[111] Geoffrey Pearson, *Hooligan: A History of Respectable Fears* (London: Macmillan, 1983), p. 74. Pearson argues that even the derivation of the term "hooligan", first coined by the popular press to describe the behaviour of gangs of rowdy youths in London during the August Bank Holiday

celebrations of 1898, is not without significance: "… it was most ingenious of late-Victorian England to disown the British hooligan by giving him an Irish name".

[112] Clive Emsley, *The English Police: A Political and Social History* (New York: Harvester Wheatsheaf, 1991), pp. 106, 179-87.